HOW TO CODE

A STEP-BY-STEP GUIDE TO COMPUTER CODING

1 2 3 4

Book 2

Max Wainewright

INFORMATION ON RESOURCES

Here's how you can find Logo and Scratch to start coding. All these resources are free of charge.

LOGO

Logo was originally designed by Seymour Papert over 40 years ago. There are various versions of it available.

If you are using a PC, you can download a free version of Logo from: **www.softronix.com/logo.html**

Alternatively you can start using Logo straight away by opening up your web browser and visiting:
http://turtleacademy.com/playground/en
or **www.calormen.com/jslogo/**

SCRATCH

You can use Scratch on a PC or Mac by opening your web browser and going to: **http://scratch.mit.edu**
Then click **'Create'** or **'Try it out'**.

There is a very similar website called 'Snap', which also works on iPads. It is available here: **http://snap.berkeley.edu/run**

If you want to run Scratch without using the web, you can download it from here:
http://scratch.mit.edu/scratch2download/

 Download our robots to use as sprites on Scratch! Go to http://www.qed-publishing.co.uk/extra-resources.php or scan this:

Design: Angela and Dave Ball, Mike Henson
Illustration: Mike Henson
Editor: Claudia Martin
Project Editor: Carly Madden
Consultant: Sean McManus
Editorial Director: Victoria Garrard
Art Director: Laura Roberts-Jensen

Copyright © QED Publishing 2015

First published in the UK in 2015 by
QED Publishing
Part of The Quarto Group
The Old Brewery,
6 Blundell Street,
London, N7 9BH

www.qed-publishing.co.uk

A catalogue record for this book is available from the British Library.

ISBN 978 1 78493 237 4

Printed in China

Scratch is developed by the Lifelong Kindergarten Group at MIT Media Lab. See http://scratch.mit.edu

For more information on Logo: www.logofoundation.org

Internet safety

Children should be supervised when using the internet, particularly when using an unfamiliar website for the first time.
The publishers and author cannot be held responsible for the content of the websites referred to in this book.

CONTENTS :: BOOK 2

Enter

INTRODUCTION

This book will show you how to become better at coding by learning how to use loops, sound and variables. We're going to use two simple and free-to-use programming languages: Logo and Scratch. For help with downloading them or finding a website where you can use them, turn to page 2. But first let's have a quick reminder about how to start coding.

What is coding?

Coding means writing a set of words or numbers that will tell a computer what to do. Coding is also called computer programming. To program a computer, we need to use the right words in the correct order.

Let's see what these instructions – or commands – will draw: **U3 R2 D2 R2**.

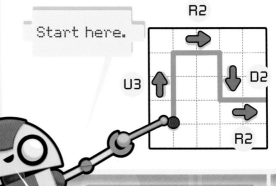

Start here.

R2

U3

D2

R2

U3 means move up 3 squares. R2 means move right 2.

fd 60 makes the turtle move forwards 60 steps.

fd 30
rt 90
fd 60
rt 90
fd 30
rt 90
fd 60

Using Logo, we can practise simple programming – like commanding the computer to draw a rectangle. **Fd 90** means 'move forward 90 steps'. **Rt 90** means 'turn right by 90 degrees' – that's a quarter turn to the right, making a right angle.

Scratch uses a similar approach to Logo, making a sprite move around the 'stage' area in the top left of the Scratch screen. But with Scratch, you drag and join your commands rather than typing them.

File▼ Edit▼ Tips About

Scripts Costumes Sounds

Motion   Events
Looks   Control
Sound   Sensing
Pen   Operators
Data   More Blocks

Move ▢ steps
Turn ↻ ▢ degrees
Turn ↺ ▢ degrees

When U▼ key pressed
point in direction 0▼
move ▢ steps

This is the scripts area – drag your commands over here. If you need to remove a command, drag it off the scripts area.

This area is called the stage.

Choose the group of commands from here.

What are loops, outputs and variables?

In the next few pages, we'll learn how to use loops to make programs repeat things over and over.

`repeat 5 [ draw_square ]`

Making a sprite or turtle move or draw is just one possible output. An output is information that a computer produces, as a result of commands we give it. In this book, we will find out how to code another output – sound.

When `e▼` key pressed

play note `64 ▼` for `0.5` beats

Q W E R

Finally we'll explore variables. Variables are a way that computer programs store pieces of data (information).

Age = 8

AGE

Key word

Code: A set of special words or blocks that tells a computer what to do.

LOOPS

Computers are very good at doing things over and over again. A loop is a way of making your program do something repetitive – like count up to 20, draw a shape with lots of sides, or make a spaceship orbit round and round a planet.

Why use loops?

Imagine you want to write a program to draw a square. You could do it like this:

1. Draw the first side.
2. Turn 90 degrees.
3. Draw the second side.
4. Turn 90 degrees.
5. Draw the third side.
6. Turn 90 degrees.
7. Draw the fourth side.
8. Turn 90 degrees.

It would take 8 separate instructions. A loop makes this much simpler. With a loop we just need 3 instructions:

1. Repeat this 4 times:
2. Draw a side.
3. Turn 90 degrees.

There must be a better way to do this!

Logo loops

We're going to write some Logo programs to try out making repeat loops. First of all, in case you're new to Logo, let's get to grips with how to use it.

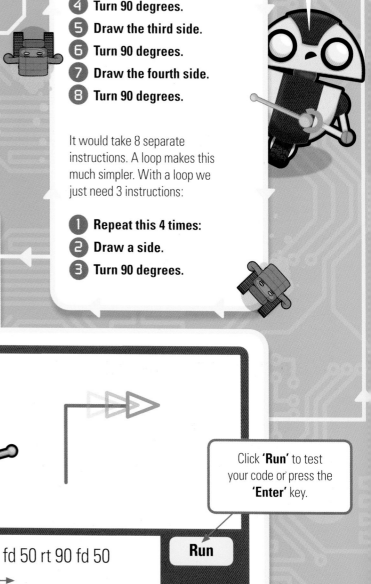

This is the drawing box. The output of your program will show up here.

Click **'Run'** to test your code or press the **'Enter'** key.

fd 50 rt 90 fd 50

Run

This is your command box. Type your program here.

Coding simple loops

Try typing this code into the Logo command box, then press **'Return'** or click **'Run'**.

```
repeat 4 [ fd 50 rt 90 ]
```
Run

How many times to repeat the commands.

Any commands between the square brackets get repeated.

Key word

Loop: A set of repeated instructions.

```
repeat 4 [ fd 50 rt 90 ]
```
Run

You have drawn a square using a loop!

Now try changing the commands inside the square brackets and experimenting with the number of times to repeat the commands. Here are some examples to get you started. What shapes do these loops draw?

① `repeat 8 [ fd 50 rt 45 ]` **Run**

② `repeat 6 [ fd 50 rt 60 ]` **Run**

③ `repeat 3 [ fd 50 rt 120 ]` **Run**

④ `repeat 3 [ fd 100 rt 120 ]` **Run**

⑤ `repeat 5 [ fd 100 rt 72 ]` **Run**

⑥ `repeat 36 [ fd 10 rt 10 ]` **Run**

⑦ `repeat 4 [ fd 100 lt 90 ]` **Run**

⑧ `repeat 20 [ fd 10 ]` **Run**

Check the answers on page 30.

Type **cs** or reload the webpage after each question to clear the screen.

Loops in everyday life

We use loops in everyday life without thinking about it. When your teacher hands out books, he or she says, 'Hand out all the books,' not, 'Hand out this book, then this book, then this book...' and so on! Your parents say, 'Eat up all your peas!' not, 'Eat that pea, then that one, then that one...!' We use words like 'each' or 'every' to give our everyday commands – it's the same as saying 'repeat 20' in a loop.

Happy birthday! Blow out each candle!

PATTERNS WITH LOOPS

In Logo, we can combine repeat loops to make patterns. We'll learn how to use just a couple of commands to make Logo perform hundreds of instructions. In Logo, measurements are made in pixels – the tiniest dots that you can see on your screen.

Practise patterns

Type the following commands to draw a small square:

`repeat 4 [ fd 20 rt 90 ]` **Run**

Now draw 8 of those squares in a line using another repeat command wrapped around the first repeat command:

`repeat 8 [ repeat 4 [ fd 20 rt 90 ] fd 25 ]` **Run**

This works because the code tells Logo:

Repeat this 8 times:
Draw a square, then move forward a bit.

This time we are going to draw 36 squares using repeat commands, but turn a small angle (10 degrees) after drawing each square:

`repeat 36 [ repeat 4 [ fd 50 rt 90 ] rt 10 ]` **Run**

You should see a pattern like this:

Now try changing your code slightly to see how the pattern changes. Experiment with different values for the size of the square, and the number of times it gets repeated.

You should see a pattern like this.

You can also use **setpc** (set pen colour) and a number to change the colour of the pattern: e.g. **setpc 5.**

How does the pattern work?

When one loop runs inside another loop like this, they are called nested loops.

repeat 36 [

repeat 4 [fd 50 rt 90]

rt 10]

The inner loop draws one square.

The outer loop repeats it 36 times, then turns right by 10 degrees.

1

Now try combining three patterns on top of each other. We'll start with a large square with a side of 120 pixels.

`repeat 36 [ repeat 4 [ fd 120 rt 90 ] rt 10 ]` **Run**

2

Now change the colour to red:

`setpc 4` **Run**

Next we are going to draw another pattern on top of the first one, with a shorter side length of 80 pixels:

`repeat 36 [ repeat 4 [ fd 80 rt 90 ] rt 10 ]` **Run**

3

Now change the colour to blue:

`setpc 1` **Run**

Finish off with a smaller square side of 60 pixels:

`repeat 36 [ repeat 4 [ fd 60 rt 90 ] rt 10 ]` **Run**

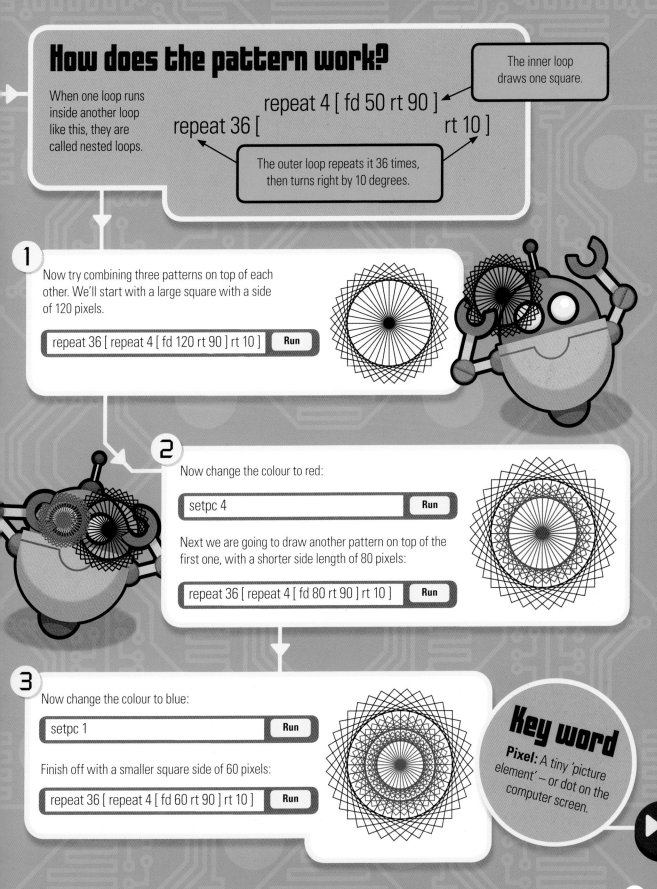

Key word

Pixel: A tiny 'picture element' – or dot on the computer screen.

LOOPS IN SCRATCH

Now we're going to look at how we can use loops in Scratch. Loops work the same way in Scratch as in Logo, but instead of typing your commands, you drag and drop them. Let's have a go.

Draw a square

If you wanted to draw a square in Logo, you would type:

repeat 4 [fd 10 rt 90]   **Run**

In Scratch, we can create the same code by dragging **'Repeat'**, **'Move'** and **'Turn'** blocks:

1 Go to the Scratch website then click **'Create'** or **'Try it out'**. Turn to page 2 for help. Now click on the **'Scripts'** tab in the centre of the Scratch screen. Choose the **Control** group.

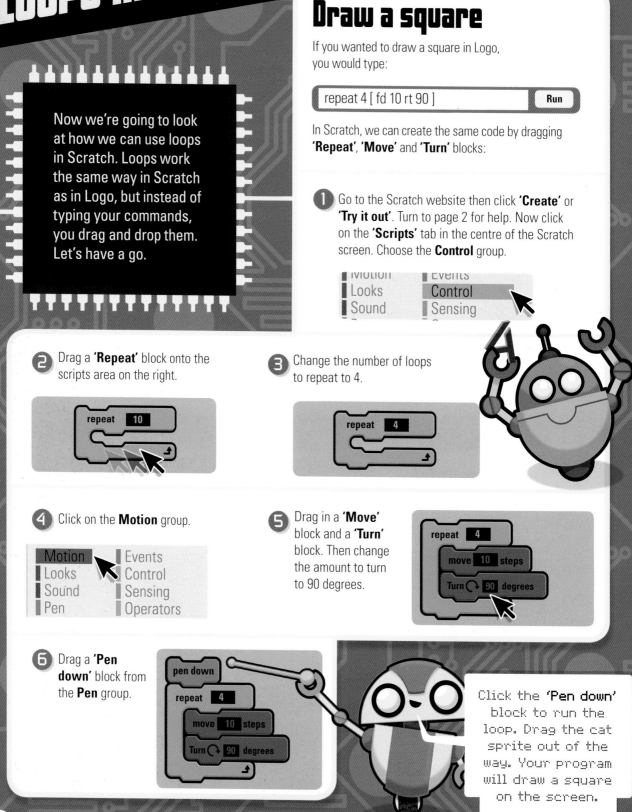

Motion   Events
Looks   Control
Sound   Sensing

2 Drag a **'Repeat'** block onto the scripts area on the right.

repeat   10

3 Change the number of loops to repeat to 4.

repeat   4

4 Click on the **Motion** group.

Motion   Events
Looks   Control
Sound   Sensing
Pen   Operators

5 Drag in a **'Move'** block and a **'Turn'** block. Then change the amount to turn to 90 degrees.

repeat   4
move   10   steps
Turn ↻ 90 degrees

6 Drag a **'Pen down'** block from the **Pen** group.

pen down
repeat   4
move   10   steps
Turn ↻ 90 degrees

Click the 'Pen down' block to run the loop. Drag the cat sprite out of the way. Your program will draw a square on the screen.

Saving your work

Click the **'File'** menu at the top of the page on the left. Then click:
New – to start some new work.
Download to your computer – to save a file on to your computer.
Upload from your computer – to open a file you have saved earlier.

Practising Scratch loops

Create these 5 loop blocks on the scripts area. You'll also need to drag over a **'Pen down'** and a **'Clear'** block.
Try clicking on the **'Pen down'** code block and then on each of the **'Repeat'** blocks in turn. Click **'Clear'** to erase
your shapes. Test out what each of the loops draws. Check the answers on page 30.

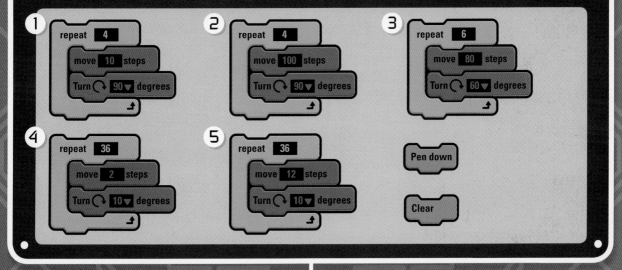

① repeat **4**
move **10** steps
Turn ⟳ **90▼** degrees

② repeat **4**
move **100** steps
Turn ⟳ **90▼** degrees

③ repeat **6**
move **80** steps
Turn ⟳ **60▼** degrees

④ repeat **36**
move **2** steps
Turn ⟳ **10▼** degrees

⑤ repeat **36**
move **12** steps
Turn ⟳ **10▼** degrees

Pen down

Clear

After drawing each of the shapes above, try dragging the Scratch sprite to a new space on the screen. You can start building up a picture or pattern.

File▼ Edit▼ Tips About

repeat **4**
move **10** steps
Turn ⟳ **90▼** degrees

repeat **4**
move **100** ste...
Turn ⟳ **90▼**

repeat **36**
move **2**
Turn ⟳ **10▼** degrees

You could draw this robot!

Do you like my new look?

LOOPS FOREVER

How to code a swimming fish

1 Start by going to the Scratch website. Delete the main sprite by right-clicking on it and then choosing **'Delete'**.

Sometimes we need loops that run forever. This is particularly useful in games where we want something to keep happening, like moving a sprite around. We're going to code a game where a fish keeps swimming around the screen, following the mouse pointer.

info
duplicate
delete

Right-clicking means press this button if you're on a PC. If you're on a Mac, press **'Control'** and click.

2 Now make your own fish sprite. Start by clicking **'Paint new sprite'**.

Select the **Ellipse** tool.

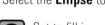 Set to fill in.

 Choose orange.

Draw a wide ellipse.

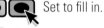

Draw more ellipses... and use the **Erase** or **Select** tool to delete the back of its tail.

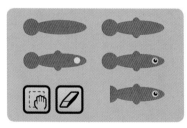

3 Now click on the **'Scripts'** tab next to the red stop button. You're going to drag some code to the scripts area to make the fish swim forward once the program starts.

Drag the **'When green flag clicked'** block from the **Events** group.

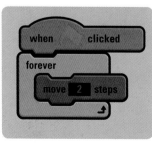

when   clicked

forever

move 2 steps

Drag the **'Forever'** loop block from the **Control** group and the **'Move'** block from the **Motion** group.

Change the **'Move...steps'** value to 2 to slow the fish down.

Click the green flag (near the top of the screen) to test your code.

4

To make the fish change direction, drag the **'Point towards'** block from the **Motion** group into the loop. Set it to 'mouse pointer'.

Test your code by clicking the green flag!

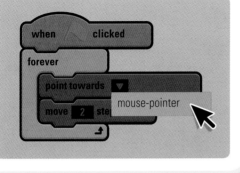

Every time the loop repeats, it makes the fish point towards the mouse pointer. It also moves it every loop. Without loops, the game wouldn't work!

Download our robots to use as sprites on Scratch! Go to http://www. qed-publishing.co.uk/extra-resources.php or scan this:

5

Now draw your own background picture for the game.

First click **'Stage'**.

Then click **'Backdrops'**.

Click the **Fill** tool and choose a blue colour. Now click the background to colour it in.

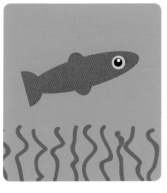

Use the **Brush** tool to draw some reeds.

Use the **Line width** slider to change the size of the reeds.

Your program is now complete! Click the green flag icon at the top of the screen to start playing.

REPEAT UNTIL...

How to code a maze game

Sometimes we need to stop loops when something happens – for example, if a player in a game bumps into a wall. To program things like this, we use a 'repeat until' loop. We are going to code a simple maze game to learn how to use this technique.

1

Start Scratch. Drag code to the scripts area to make the Scratch sprite move slowly across the screen, pointing towards the mouse pointer.

```
when          clicked
repeat until
    point towards    mouse-pointer ▼
    move    1    steps
```

For help, see steps 3 and 4 on pages 12–13. But use a **'Repeat until'** block instead of a **'Forever'** block.

Change the speed of the sprite to move 1 step each loop.

2

Make the Scratch sprite smaller by clicking the **Shrink** icon at the top of the screen, and then clicking the Scratch sprite several times.

3

To make the sprite start in the same place each time, drag the **'Set x to'** and **'Set y to'** code blocks from the **Motion** group to the scripts area.

Experiment with changing the **'Set x'** and **'Set y'** values.

```
when          clicked
set x to    -200
set y to    100
repeat until
    point towards    mouse-pointer ▼
    move    1    steps
```

Ow!

Click the green flag to test your code.

Set x and y coordinates

`set x to -200`

'Set x to' tells Scratch how far to place the sprite to the left or right of the screen.

`set y to 100`

'Set y to' tells Scratch how far to place the sprite up or down the screen.

(-200,100)

4

Draw a simple background for the game. Look at step 5 on page 13 for help getting started.

Use the **Rectangle** tool to draw some walls. Make them all the same colour.

wall

5

The **'Repeat until'** block will loop forever because we haven't told it when to stop yet. It needs to repeat until the sprite touches a brown colour – the wall colour.

Sprites

Sprite1

Click on the Scratch sprite icon and then the **'Scripts'** tab to bring your code back.

Events
Control
Sensing
Operators
More Blocks

Click the **Sensing** group.

`repeat until` `touching color ?`
`point towards mouse-pointer`
`move 1 steps`

Drag a **'Touching color'** block onto the top of the **'Repeat until'** block.

`touching color ?`

Click the coloured square then choose the colour to check for...

...by clicking one of the walls.

`repeat until` `touching color ?`

Now your game will play until the sprite hits a wall. Test it by clicking the green flag at the top of the screen. To play again, drag your sprite away from the wall.

Eeeeek!

We're going to practise using 'repeat until' loops by creating another game. This will have two sprite objects, the Scratch cat sprite and a dog, which will chase after the cat. The player will control the cat, moving it around the screen until it is caught.

1

How to code a chase game

Drag code to the scripts area to make the Scratch sprite move slowly across the screen, pointing towards the mouse pointer.

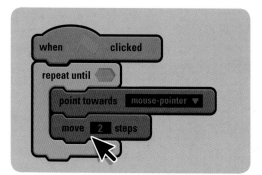

Look at steps 3 and 4 on pages 12–13 for help. Remember to use the **'Repeat until'** loop. Change the speed of the sprite to move 2 steps each loop.

2

Make the Scratch sprite smaller by clicking the **Shrink** icon at the top of the screen, and then clicking the Scratch sprite several times.

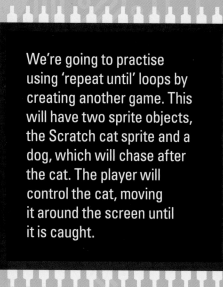

Pick me!

Click the green flag at the top of the screen to test your code.

3

Now add the second sprite.

Click this icon to choose a new sprite from the library.

Then scroll down to the **dog** and click on it.

OK Click **'OK'**.

Use the **Shrink** icon to make the dog smaller.

Pick me!

Pick me!

4

Now we will make the dog sprite move.

Sprites

Sprite1   Dog2

Click the **dog** so the code you are about to build will control the dog rather than the cat!

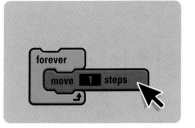

Drag in a **'Forever'** loop block from the **Control** group. Add a **'Move'** block. Set it to 1 step each loop.

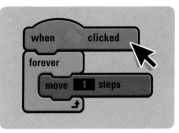

From the **Events** group, drag a **'When green flag clicked'** block over. Put it at the top of the code.

After step 4, test your code. The cat should follow the mouse pointer. The dog should move in a straight line forever – this means it might get stuck on the right side of the screen. Just drag it to the left!

5

To make the dog chase the cat, click the **dog** sprite.

Sprites

Sprite1   Dog2

From the **Motion** group, drag on a **'Point towards'** code block. Set it to 'Sprite1'.

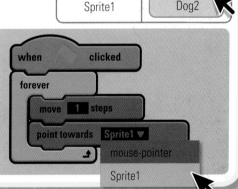

6

Now the most important part – making the 'until' part of the 'repeat until' loop! The aim is to keep the cat moving until the dog catches it.

Sprites

Sprite1   Dog2

Click the **cat** sprite.

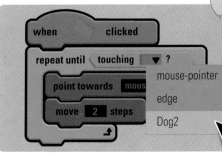

Drag a **'Touching'** code block from the top of the **Sensing** group and set it to 'Dog2'.

Now click the green flag and start to play your game!

ADDING SOUND

Our code so far has used two different inputs: pressing keys and moving the mouse. Our outputs have all been on screen. We are now going to learn how to control another sort of output – sound.

Getting started with sound in Scratch

Click the **Sound** group.

```
play note  60 ▼  for  0.5  beats
```

Drag a **'Play note'** code block onto the scripts area and try clicking it.

Key word
Output: The information produced by a computer, such as sound or movements of the sprite.

Changing beats

```
play note  60 ▼  for  2  beats
```

Try changing the value in the 'beats' box to 2. Click the code block.

```
play note  60 ▼  for  0.25  beats
```

Now change it to a small number – 0.25 (a quarter of a beat). Click it.

The bigger the number, the longer the note is played. Experiment!

Changing the note

Change how high or low the note is by changing the value in the 'note' box.

Either type a number in, or choose a note from the keyboard.

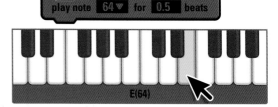

```
play note  64 ▼  for  0.5  beats
```

E(64)

The higher the number, the higher the note. The lower the number, the lower the note.

You may not be able to hear notes much below 20, or above 100 – but your dog might!

Creating a tune

Drag a few **'Play note'** code blocks onto the scripts area and change their note values.

Click the top one to play all the notes. Experiment to make your own tune!

```
play note  64 ▼  for  0.5  beats
play note  62 ▼  for  0.5  beats
play note  60 ▼  for  0.5  beats
play note  60 ▼  for  0.5  beats
```

Make a piano program

1 Click the **Events** group.

> Events
> Control

2 Drag a **'When key pressed'** code block onto the scripts area and set it to 'q'.

```
When  q ▼  key pressed
    o
    p
    q
    r  ▼
```

3 Click the **Sound** group.

> Motion   Eve
> Looks   Co
> Sound   Ser
> Pen   Ope
> Data   Me

4 Drag a **'Play note'** code block onto the **'When key pressed'** code block, so the note will be played when the 'q' key is pressed.

```
When  q ▼  key pressed
play note  60 ▼  for  0.5  beats
```

5 Repeat steps 1 to 4 to create more blocks of code. Then change the value of the keys that they will respond to, and the notes they will play, so they look like this:

```
When  q ▼  key pressed
play note  60 ▼  for  0.5  beats

When  w ▼  key pressed
play note  62 ▼  for  0.5  beats

When  e ▼  key pressed
play note  64 ▼  for  0.5  beats
```

> Add more **'When key pressed'** blocks to complete your piano. You can experiment with the **'Set instrument'** block to change the sound.

SOUND EFFECTS

The previous pages looked at how we could make sound using code. We are now going to look at how we can use sound within loops, and how to add sound effects to games.

Create a drum machine

We can combine sound effects with loops to make a simple drum machine.

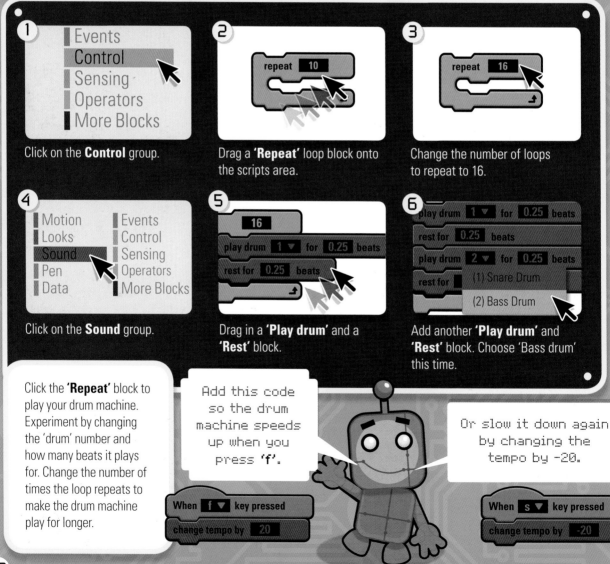

1. Click on the **Control** group.

   Events
   Control
   Sensing
   Operators
   More Blocks

2. Drag a **'Repeat'** loop block onto the scripts area.

   repeat 10

3. Change the number of loops to repeat to 16.

   repeat 16

4. Click on the **Sound** group.

   Motion   Events
   Looks   Control
   Sound   Sensing
   Pen   Operators
   Data   More Blocks

5. Drag in a **'Play drum'** and a **'Rest'** block.

   16
   play drum 1 ▼ for 0.25 beats
   rest for 0.25 beats

6. Add another **'Play drum'** and **'Rest'** block. Choose 'Bass drum' this time.

   play drum 1 ▼ for 0.25 beats
   rest for 0.25 beats
   play drum 2 ▼ for 0.25 beats
   rest for
   (1) Snare Drum
   (2) Bass Drum

Click the **'Repeat'** block to play your drum machine. Experiment by changing the 'drum' number and how many beats it plays for. Change the number of times the loop repeats to make the drum machine play for longer.

Add this code so the drum machine speeds up when you press **'f'**.

Or slow it down again by changing the tempo by -20.

When f ▼ key pressed
change tempo by 20

When s ▼ key pressed
change tempo by -20

Add sound to your games

Games can be a lot more fun if they have sound effects. We are going to learn how to add sound to the games we made in the previous pages.

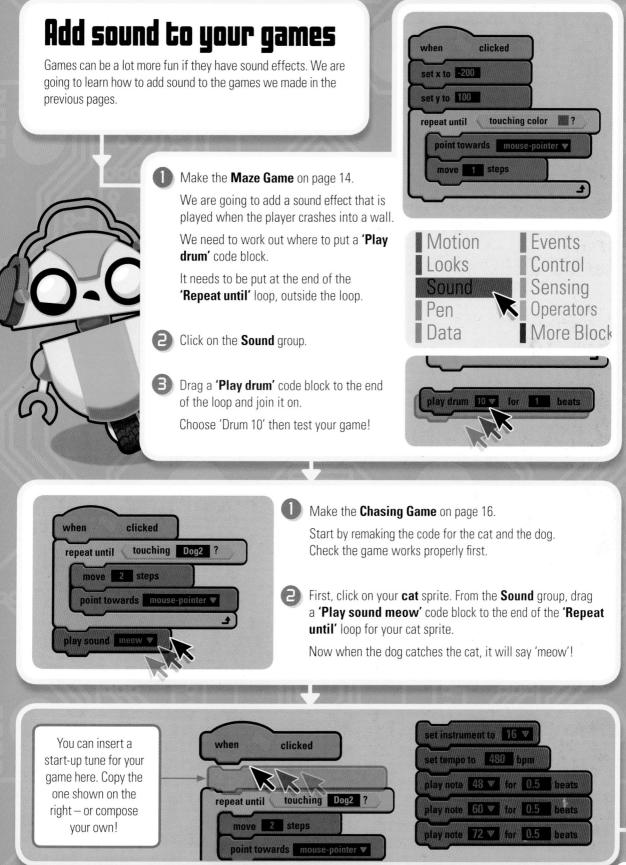

1. Make the **Maze Game** on page 14.

   We are going to add a sound effect that is played when the player crashes into a wall.

   We need to work out where to put a **'Play drum'** code block.

   It needs to be put at the end of the **'Repeat until'** loop, outside the loop.

2. Click on the **Sound** group.

3. Drag a **'Play drum'** code block to the end of the loop and join it on.

   Choose 'Drum 10' then test your game!

```
when      clicked
set x to -200
set y to 100
repeat until   touching color   ?
    point towards   mouse-pointer ▼
    move   1   steps
```

Motion	Events
Looks	Control
Sound	Sensing
Pen	Operators
Data	More Block

```
play drum  10 ▼  for  1  beats
```

1. Make the **Chasing Game** on page 16.

   Start by remaking the code for the cat and the dog. Check the game works properly first.

2. First, click on your **cat** sprite. From the **Sound** group, drag a **'Play sound meow'** code block to the end of the **'Repeat until'** loop for your cat sprite.

   Now when the dog catches the cat, it will say 'meow'!

```
when      clicked
repeat until   touching   Dog2  ?
    move   2   steps
    point towards   mouse-pointer ▼
play sound  meow ▼
```

You can insert a start-up tune for your game here. Copy the one shown on the right – or compose your own!

```
when      clicked

repeat until   touching   Dog2  ?
    move   2   steps
    point towards   mouse-pointer ▼
```

```
set instrument to  16 ▼
set tempo to  480  bpm
play note  48 ▼  for  0.5  beats
play note  60 ▼  for  0.5  beats
play note  72 ▼  for  0.5  beats
```

VARIABLES

Variables are a way that computer programs store pieces of data or information. They can be used to store things like your name, the score in a game or how big a shape is. Unlike normal numbers, variables can change their value when something happens.

Storing something in a variable

Most computer programming languages store values in variables in a similar way:

set age = 8
or
age = 8

They tell the computer that it needs to store the value 8 in a special box called 'age'.

A variable is a bit like a special box...

...that has something important stored inside.

What can variables be used for?

After a program has stored a value in a variable, it can be used by another part of the program. One part of the program might show the value of the variable to the person using it – as when the score is shown during a game. Or the program might do something if the value of a variable reaches a certain number – such as say, "Well done!"

Ah! The score is 100. Time to stop the game – I'm off for a byte to eat!

Using variables in Scratch

Key word
Variable: A way that computer programs store information.

1

Click on the **Data** group.

Sound | Sensing
Pen | Operators
Data | More Bloc

2

Click '**Make a Variable**'.

Data | More B...

Make a Variable

3

Give the variable the name 'a'. Then click '**OK**'.

New Variable

Variable name: **a**

● For all sprites   ○ For this

OK

4

Drag the '**Change a by 1**' code block to the scripts area.

change a ▼ by 1

5

Click on the code block you dragged in. You should see the value of the variable change in the top left corner of the stage.

a   1

change a ▼ by 1

Keep clicking and it should keep going up!

Challenge

Try putting a '**Change a by 1**' code block inside a '**Repeat**' loop to make your variable count up to 20... or 100... or 500!

1...2...3... 4...5...6... 98...99...100

KEEPING SCORE

How to code a deadly shark game

We are going to make another chasing game, this time with the player avoiding a shark for as long as possible. We will use a variable to count how long the player avoids the shark, and use this variable as the score.

1 Start Scratch. Delete the main sprite and create your own fish sprite.

Shrink the fish.

For help, see steps 1 and 2 on page 12.

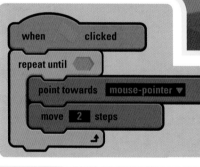

Sprite1

2 We will create code to make the fish swim towards the mouse pointer.

See pages 12–13 for help – but remember to use a **'Repeat until'** loop instead of a **'Forever'** loop.

Change the amount moved to 2 steps.

Click the green flag to test your code.

```
when       clicked
repeat until
    point towards   mouse-pointer ▼
    move   2   steps
```

3

Start to make a shark to chase the fish by clicking **'Paint new sprite'**.

Choose a colour and select the **Ellipse** tool. Draw a narrow ellipse.

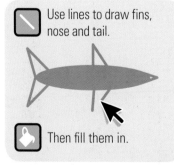

Use lines to draw fins, nose and tail.

Then fill them in.

Add an eye.

If you make a mistake, use the **Undo** button.

Use the **Shrink** button to make the shark sprite smaller.

24

4

Now we will make a variable to keep the score.

Sound
Pen
Data

Make a Variable

Variable name: **s**

OK

Click on the **Data** group.

Click '**Make a Variable**'.

Call it 's' (for score).

Then click '**OK**'.

5

Click your **fish** sprite so we can add more code to it.

Sprites

i

Sprite1   Sprite2

6

The score needs to go up as the fish swims around.

Drag a '**Change s by 1**' code block from the **Data** group into the loop here.

Click the green flag to test your code.

The score in the top left of the stage should keep going up.

s   724

when   clicked
repeat until
  change   s ▼ by 1
  point towards   mouse-pointer ▼
  move   2   steps

7

The score must be reset each time the game is played. Drag a '**Set s to 0**' code block into your program before the start of the loop.

when   clicked
set   s ▼ to   0
repeat until

8

Next we will make the game stop when the shark catches the fish. From the **Sensing** group, drag a '**Touching**' code block onto the '**Repeat until**' loop. Set it to 'Sprite2'.

set   s ▼ to   0
repeat until   touching   ▼ ?
  change   s ▼ by 1   mouse-pointer
  point towards   mouse   edge
  move   2   steps   Sprite2

9

when   clicked
forever
  point towards   Sprite1 ▼
  move   1   st   mouse-pointer
                   Sprite1

Double-click the **shark** sprite so you can add code to control it. Copy the code on the left, which will make the shark chase your fish. See step 5 on page 17 for extra hints.

Now test your game!

Move the sprites apart to start a new game.

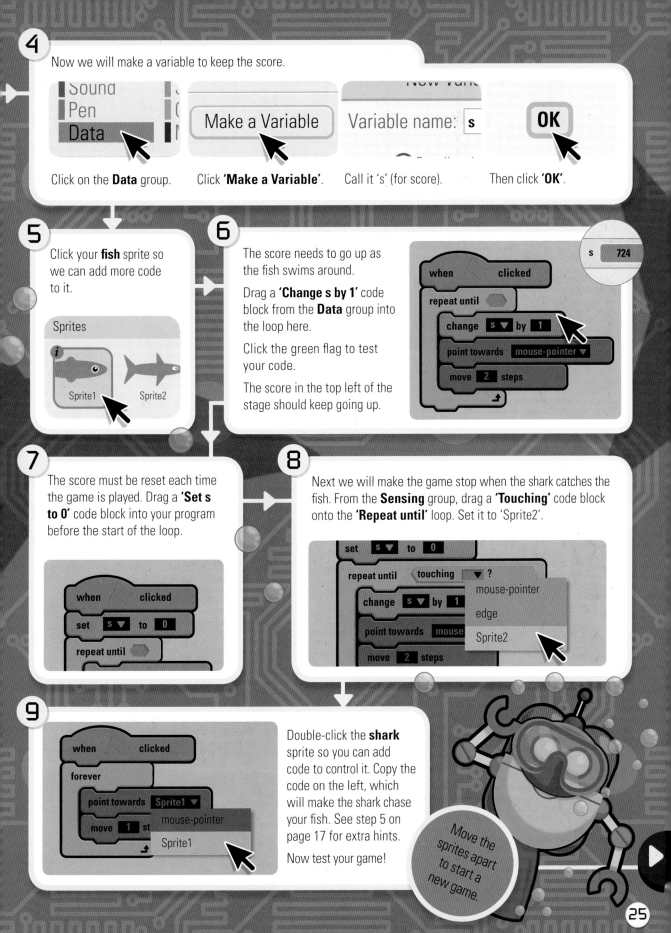

COUNTING CLICKS

Now we're going to learn how to use a variable to count mouse clicks. We will make a game where the player has to pat the cat as it moves across the screen. We need a variable to count the number of times the cat is patted. At the end of the game, the score will be shown.

Pat me if you can!

How to code a pat the cat game

1

Make a variable to keep the score.

Sound	
Pen	
Data	

Make a Variable

New Varie...

Variable name: **s**   **OK**

Click on the **Data** group.   Click **'Make a Variable'**.   Call it 's' (for score).   Then click **'OK'**.

2

We will create a loop to move the cat. From the **Events** group, drag the **'When green flag clicked'** block. Drag a **'Repeat until'** block from the **Control** group and a **'Move'** block from the **Motion** group.

Change the **'Move...steps'** value to 5 to slow down the cat.

3

The score must go up when the cat is clicked.

Click on the **Events** group. Drag the **'When this sprite clicked'** block to the scripts area.

Click on the **Data** group. Drag the **'Change s by 1'** code block to join it.

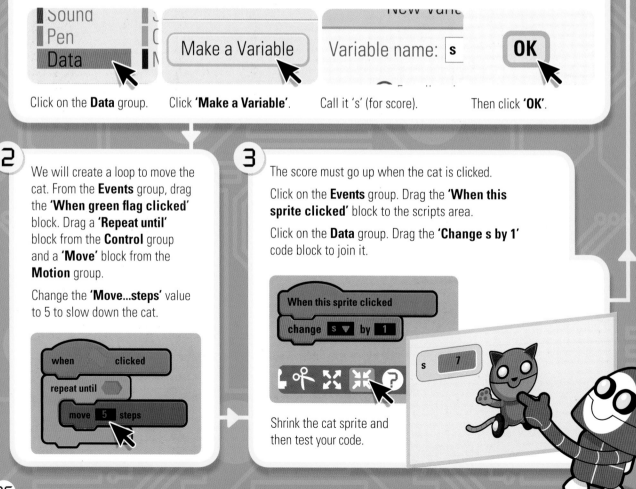

Shrink the cat sprite and then test your code.

4

To make the cat start in the same place each time, we need to click on the **Motion** group.

Drag over a **'Set x to'** code block and drop it before the loop starts.

Set the 'x' value to -180.

See page 15 if you need help using **'Set x to'**.

```
when    clicked
set x to -180
repeat until
    move 5 steps
```

5

Every time we play the game, the score needs to go back to 0.

We need to add code telling Scratch to **'Set s to 0'** when the green flag is clicked to start the game.

Motion
Looks
Sound
Pen
Data

Click the **Data** group.

```
when    clicked
set s ▼ to 0
set x to -180
repeat until
```

Drag on a **'Set s to 0'** block.

6

Next we will make the cat stop at the screen edge.

Control
Sensing
Operators
More Blocks

Click on the **Sensing** group.

```
set x to -180
repeat until  touching ▼ ?
    move 5 steps
                mouse-pointer
                edge
```

Drag a **'Touching'** code block onto the **'Repeat until'** loop – and click 'edge'.

7

Finally, we would like to display the score at the end of the game.

Motion
Looks
Sound

Click on the **Looks** group.

say Hello!

Drag a **'Say...'** code block to the end of the **'Repeat until'** loop.

Sound
Pen
Data

Click on the **Data** group.

say s

Drag the **'s'** code block onto the **'Say...'** block to display the score.

Click this button to make the game larger.

Challenge

Can you add sound effects to your game? Make the cat say 'meow' every time you click it.

DEBUGGING

Coding can be a process of trial and error – testing ideas and seeing if they work. It is normal to make mistakes! A bug is another name for a mistake in a piece of code that stops it from working properly. Debugging means fixing those mistakes. Try these debugging exercises.

Key word

Debugging: Getting rid of mistakes that stop your code from working properly.

1 Debug this Logo code so it draws a square using a repeat loop.

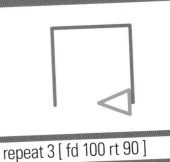

repeat 3 [fd 100 rt 90]

2 Now fix this Logo code so it draws a square, too.

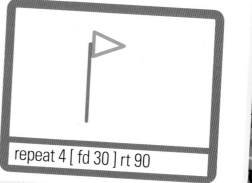

repeat 4 [fd 30] rt 90

Debugging tips

When your code doesn't do what you want it to:

1 Work through your code step by step, thinking about what each command does.

2 Draw a picture or diagram to help.

3 Have a break for a few minutes!

3 This Scratch code has a bug in it. Fix it so it draws a square.

pen down

move 10 steps

repeat 4

turn ↻ 90 degrees

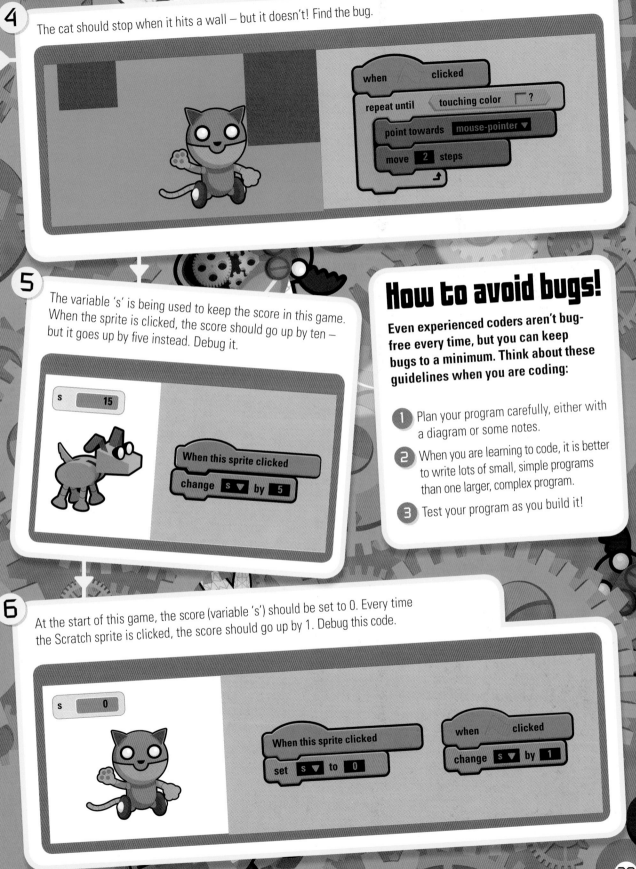

4 The cat should stop when it hits a wall — but it doesn't! Find the bug.

```
when    clicked
repeat until    touching color    ?
    point towards    mouse-pointer ▾
    move   2   steps
```

5 The variable 's' is being used to keep the score in this game. When the sprite is clicked, the score should go up by ten — but it goes up by five instead. Debug it.

s   15

```
When this sprite clicked
change   s ▾   by   5
```

How to avoid bugs!

Even experienced coders aren't bug-free every time, but you can keep bugs to a minimum. Think about these guidelines when you are coding:

1 Plan your program carefully, either with a diagram or some notes.

2 When you are learning to code, it is better to write lots of small, simple programs than one larger, complex program.

3 Test your program as you build it!

6 At the start of this game, the score (variable 's') should be set to 0. Every time the Scratch sprite is clicked, the score should go up by 1. Debug this code.

s   0

```
When this sprite clicked
set   s ▾   to   0
```

```
when    clicked
change   s ▾   by   1
```

ANSWERS

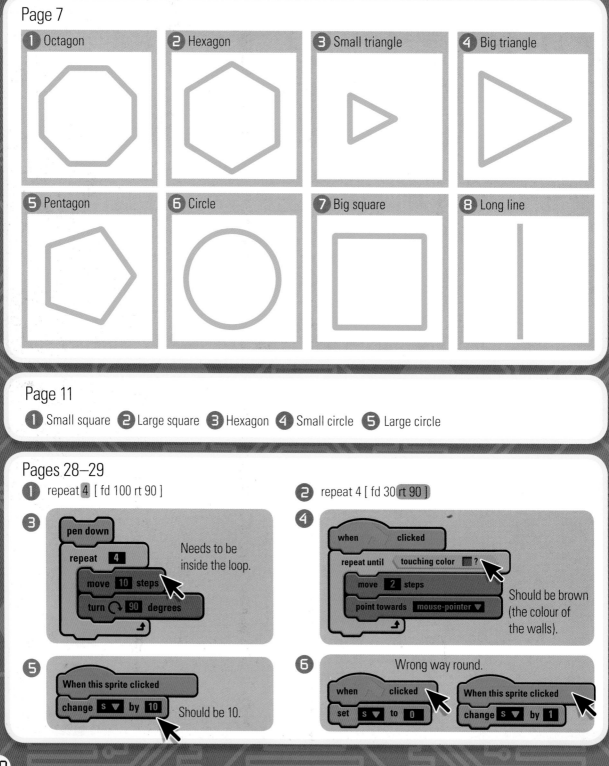

Page 7

1 Octagon
2 Hexagon
3 Small triangle
4 Big triangle
5 Pentagon
6 Circle
7 Big square
8 Long line

Page 11

1 Small square 2 Large square 3 Hexagon 4 Small circle 5 Large circle

Pages 28–29

1 repeat 4 [fd 100 rt 90]

2 repeat 4 [fd 30 rt 90]

3
```
pen down
repeat    4
    move  10  steps
    turn ↻ 90 degrees
```
Needs to be inside the loop.

4
```
when       clicked
repeat until    touching color   ?
    move  2  steps
    point towards   mouse-pointer ▼
```
Should be brown (the colour of the walls).

5
```
When this sprite clicked
change  s ▼  by  10
```
Should be 10.

6 Wrong way round.
```
when       clicked
set  s ▼  to  0
```
```
When this sprite clicked
change  s ▼  by  1
```

Download our robots to use as sprites on Scratch!

Go to http://www.qed-publishing.co.uk/extra-resources.php or scan this:

Browser

www.qed-publishing.co.uk/extra-resources.php

Other books in the *How to Code* series:

BOOK 1

Introduction to the basic principles of coding. Experiment with Logo and Scratch. Move turtles and sprites across the screen!
ISBN: 978 1 78493 236 7

BOOK 3

Take coding further by learning about selection with 'if' statements. Code a simple quiz in Python or make a sandwich for a robot!
ISBN: 978 1 78493 238 1

BOOK 4

Develop your coding techniques further by learning how to create web pages using HTML. Discover how to program in JavaScript. Build a website about pets!
ISBN: 978 1 78493 239 8

HOW TO CODE – THE GROWN-UPS' GUIDE

A handbook for parents and teachers, which provides background information and detailed explanations on all topics covered in Books 1–4.
ISBN: 978 1 78493 240 4

GLOSSARY

Code A set of commands or blocks that tells a computer what to do.

Command A word or code-block that tells the computer what to do.

Co-ordinates A set of numbers that gives the position of a point. It is common to use two numbers, called x and y. X gives the distance to the right or left of the screen. Y gives the distance up or down.

Data Information that can be stored and used by a computer.

Debugging Fixing problems (bugs) in a computer program.

Degree The unit of measurement for angles. If we turn all the way around, we turn 360 degrees.

Download To copy data from one computer system to another, using the internet.

Event Something that happens while a program is running, for example a key being pressed, or the program starting.

Input An action (such as pressing a key) that tells a program to do something.

Language A system of words, numbers, symbols and rules for writing programs.

Logo A computer language in which commands move a turtle around the screen to draw.

Loop A sequence of commands repeated a number of times.

Output Something that a computer program does to show the results of a program, such as moving a sprite or making a sound.

Pixel A unit of measurement used in computing. A pixel is the smallest dot you can see on your screen.

Program The special commands that tell a computer how to do something.

Scratch A computer language that uses blocks to make programs.

Scripts area In Scratch, this is the area to the right of the Scratch screen, where you need to drag your code blocks to.

Sprite An object that moves around the screen.

Stage In Scratch, this is the area to the top left of the Scratch screen, where you can watch your sprites move about.

Turtle A robot, sprite or arrow that can be programmed to move around the floor or the computer screen.

Variable A value or piece of data stored by a computer program.

INDEX